simply relevant

{SAVOR THE MOMENTS}

Relational Bible Series for Women

Loveland, Colorado

simply relevant

{SAVOR THE MOMENTS}

Relational Bible Series for Women

Credits

Author: Amber Van Schooneveld
Executive Editor: Amy Nappa
Copy Editor: Janis Sampson and Ardeth Carlson
Chief Creative Officer: Joani Schultz
Art Director and Cover Art Director: Andrea Filer
Senior Designer: Kari K. Monson
Print Production: Eric Anderson and Shelly Dillon
Production Manager: DeAnne Lear
Photos on pages 10, 17, 23, 24, 35, 40, 42, 47, 51, 57, 68, 73 © photos.com

Unless otherwise indicated, all Scripture quotations are taken from the *Holy Bible*, New Living Translation, copyright © 1996, 2004. Used by permission of Tyndale House Publishers, Inc., Carol Stream, Illinois 60188. All rights reserved.

ISBN 978-0-7644-3889-9
10 9 8 7 6 5 4 3 2 1   18 17 16 15 14 13 12 11 10 09
Printed in the United States of America.

Contents

Welcome to Simply Relevant: Savor the Moments! This is your totally relevant six-week Bible series that will help you develop relationships with other women as you grow in your relationship with God.

Most of us will admit that we could use a little help with patience. This series will help you and your friends learn more about God's patience for you, and how he can transform us to flourish in this fruit of the Spirit.

Each week you'll find what the Bible has to say about patience and how it applies to your life. You'll learn about how God is patient; about how you can gain God's patience through the Holy Spirit; and about patience in the grocery store, in the traffic jams, in your relationships, and in God's timing… which often doesn't seem to be ours!

You can do this Bible series with five to 50 women—or even more! And you want women to really grow in relationships with one another, so always form small groups of four or five for discussion if you have a larger group. Women at any place in their faith journeys can feel right at home with this Bible series. The discussion questions can be understood and applied by women who don't know Jesus yet or women who are long-time friends with him. All the Bible passages are printed out for you, so those who aren't familiar with the Bible have the verses right in front of them.

So what will you be doing each week? Here's the structure of the sessions:

Note to the Hostess

Your hostess will be the woman facilitating your Bible series. She'll read the session through before the meeting, prepare for the activities, gather any supplies needed, and get the snacks ready. This box contains special tips just for the hostess, such as supplies to gather for the Experience, the atmosphere for the week, and ideas for snacks.

Mingling

Each week, you're going to start with snacks, mingling, and a short prayer. And this is key: Take time to share how you did with your previous week's commitment.

Experience

Together each week you'll engage in an experience that will bring a new depth of meaning to the topic you'll explore. The experiences will get every woman involved and having fun. There might be a little bit of preparation or supplies needed, which the hostess will supply.

The Word

Each week you'll read Scripture passages together and then discuss what they mean with questions from this guide. The questions are surprising, personal, and relevant to women today.

A Closer Look

This is a quick look at the Bible passages you'll be digging into each week. They'll help you develop a deeper understanding of the verses at hand while discussing their meaning in your lives. You can read them together during your session or on your own at home.

Take Action

This is where women put faith into action. You'll all commit to apply what you've learned in a practical way in the coming week. You can write your own commitment or choose from the suggested commitments. Then next week you'll check in with one another to see how you did.

Prayer

At the end of each session, you'll spend time in prayer together. You can ask for prayer requests and also pray about the commitments you've made for the upcoming week. We've also given you a verse to read together to focus your minds for prayer.

Girlfriend Time

If you want some more hangout time together after your session is over, we've given you fun suggestions for easy activities to do together to reinforce the session's topic or to just relax. This is an optional bonus that will help you grow deeper in your friendships.

Still Thirsty?

If you want to explore the week's topic more, we've given you additional verses and reflection questions to read and consider in the coming week.

We pray that in the next six weeks, this experience will help you grow as friends together, learn more about the patience God has for you, and most of all, grow closer in your relationship with Jesus.

—Group's Women's Ministry Team

Music is a great tool in creating ambience for your meeting area. Play music before and after your gathering. We recommend the *Music of Sweet Life Café*, which features songs related to many of the themes you'll explore in this Bible study. You can find it at group.com or at your local Christian bookstore.

Slow to Anger

Learning About God's Patience

Note to the Hostess:

Since this is the first meeting where your friends will be learning more about patience, go the extra mile to create an atmosphere that will be relaxing for women. They may be coming from screaming babies, demanding bosses, or road-ragers…things that don't exactly induce patience and rest.

Create a haven of tranquility with low lighting, a few flickering candles, and soft music. Serve comforting, relaxing snacks, such as chamomile tea—to soothe the nerves after a busy day—and sugar cookies.

You'll be guiding women through the Experience, so read through this section before your session.

Get It...Got It?...Good.

- comforting, relaxing snacks, like chamomile tea and sugar cookies
- flickering candles
- piece of newsprint taped to the wall, with a line drawn down the middle, and a marker for the Experience

Mingling

Enjoy the snacks the hostess has set out, and make sure you all know one another's names. Need a little help? Here's a conversation starter:

Hi, my name's [your name],
and the thing that tests my patience the most is [_____].

Before starting, make sure to pray something like this:

God, thank you for bringing each individual woman here tonight. Help us to put aside everything that's crowding our minds so that we can learn about your patience for us. In Jesus' name, amen.

Experience

(Note: The hostess will prepare this experience.) Often when people think of the God of the Old Testament, they don't think of patience; they think of a curmudgeony old man with a big beard. Do this experience to find out what women's gut thoughts about God are.

Have a piece of newsprint hanging on the wall and a marker handy. Say: *Think about the God of the Old Testament, of the flood and Noah, and of the Ten Commandments. What words or images come immediately to your mind? Be honest!"*

Have women call out their responses, and write them on the left-hand side of the paper.

Then have different women read the following verses aloud to the group.

Exodus 34:6

"The Lord passed in front of Moses, calling out, 'Yahweh! The Lord! The God of compassion and mercy! I am slow to anger and filled with unfailing love and faithfulness.'"

Psalm 86:15

"But you, O Lord, are a God of compassion and mercy, slow to get angry and filled with unfailing love and faithfulness."

Psalm 145:8

"The Lord is merciful and compassionate, slow to get angry and filled with unfailing love."

Have women call out the key words that describe God in these verses, and write these on the right-hand side of the paper. Then discuss:

Q: What impressions do you have of God that led you to say what you did on the left?

Q: When you think of God, is *patient* a word that would come to your mind? Why or why not?

Q: How do you balance your understanding of both God's anger and his patience?

the Word

Read Nehemiah 9:17-19, 26-31, and 2 Peter 3:9 together.

Nehemiah 9:17-19, 26-31

But you are a God of forgiveness, gracious and merciful, slow to become angry, and rich in unfailing love. You did not abandon them, even when they made an idol shaped like a calf and said, 'This is your god who brought you out of Egypt!' They committed terrible blasphemies.

But in your great mercy you did not abandon them to die in the wilderness. The pillar of cloud still led them forward by day, and the pillar of fire showed them the way through the night.

But despite all this, they were disobedient and rebelled against you. They turned their backs on your Law, they killed your prophets who warned them to return to you, and they committed terrible blasphemies. So you handed them over to their enemies, who made them suffer. But in their time of trouble they cried to you, and you heard them from heaven. In your great mercy, you sent them liberators who rescued them from their enemies.

But as soon as they were at peace, your people again committed evil in your sight, and once more you let their enemies conquer them. Yet whenever your people turned and cried to you again for help, you listened once more from heaven. In your wonderful mercy, you rescued them many times.

They stubbornly turned their backs on you and refused to listen. In your love, you were patient with them for many years. You sent your Spirit, who warned them through the prophets. But still they wouldn't listen! So once again you allowed the peoples of the land to conquer them. But in your great mercy, you did not destroy them completely or abandon them forever. What a gracious and merciful God you are!

2 Peter 3:9

The Lord isn't really being slow about his promise, as some people think. No, he is being patient for your sake. He does not want anyone to be destroyed, but wants everyone to repent.

a closer look

What does patience mean? Many of the passages in the Bible that speak about God's patience with his people also describe God as compassionate, forgiving, slow to anger, kind, gracious, and rich in love. (Exodus 34:6; Numbers 14:18; Nehemiah 9; Psalms 86:15, 103:8, and 145:8)

Patience is more than just not getting testy while waiting for something. Patience is something much grander. Patience is the manifestation of God's compassion, his forgiveness, his grace, and his rich, abounding love.

scripture discussion questions

In groups of four or five, discuss these questions:

Q: Nehemiah 9 tells about God's reaction to the Israelites' disobedience—both his punishment of them and his patience. What is the overall impression you are left with of God's character?

Q: Why do you think God was so patient with the Israelites, forgiving them over and over?

Q: Read 2 Peter 3:9 again. What is the difference between God's patience in the Old Testament and in the New Testament?

Q: Why is God patient with you? Really unpack this. Think of all the reasons you can.

Q: Do you think God has been patient with you in your own life? If so, give examples.

Q: How does thinking about God's patience change your view of God?

Q: In light of God's patience, does it change the way you think about being patient yourself? How?

Take Action

Let's not just *talk* about God's patience, *let's do it!* Write below how you're going to reflect on and experience God's patience this week. If you're having a hard time thinking of something, choose one of the ideas below. Next week you'll share with one another how you did.

this week

○ I'm going to experience and dwell in God's patience this week by:

....

....

....

....

○ I'm going to read all the verses listed in A Closer Look and Still Thirsty? and meditate on them.

○ I'm going to list all the times in my life I've experienced God's patience and spend time thanking God for his patience.

○ Each time my patience is tested, I'm going to reflect on God's character: his compassion, grace, love, and slowness to anger.

Prayer

End your time together in prayer to your Father. Read 1 Timothy 1:16 together:

> But God had mercy on me so that Christ Jesus could use me as a prime example of his great patience with even the worst sinners. Then others will realize that they, too, can believe in him and receive eternal life.

God's patience for us is unlimited. Thank God for his unending patience for you, his compassion and love and grace. Ask him to transform your minds to think rightly of him, as a God who is slow to anger and abounding in love for you.

Girlfriend Time

If you want to spend more time together with your girlfriends, spend some time sharing stories of God's patience for you in your own life—share with one another your journey with God, starting from the beginning, and all the instances God has shown himself to be merciful, slow to anger, and patient with you.

Still Thirsty?

If you're still thirsty to know more about God's patience, check out these Scriptures.

1 Timothy 1:15-16

"This is a trustworthy saying, and everyone should accept it: 'Christ Jesus came into the world to save sinners'—and I am the worst of them all. But God had mercy on me so that Christ Jesus could use me as a prime example of his great patience with even the worst sinners. Then others will realize that they, too, can believe in him and receive eternal life."

Q: When have you felt like a "prime example" of God's patience?

Q: Can you think of a time God has shown you patience so you could be an example for those who might believe in him?

2 Peter 3:15

"And remember, the Lord's patience gives people time to be saved. This is what our beloved brother Paul also wrote to you with the wisdom God gave him."

Q: Do you usually equate patience with salvation? Take time to deeply reflect on this concept.

Romans 9:21-24

"When a potter makes jars out of clay, doesn't he have a right to use the same lump of clay to make one jar for decoration and another to throw garbage into? In the same way, even though God has the right to show his anger and his power, he is very patient with those on whom his anger falls, who are destined for destruction. He does this to make the riches of his glory shine even brighter on those to whom he shows mercy, who were prepared in advance for glory. And we are among those whom he selected, both from the Jews and from the Gentiles."

Q: How is God's glory shown not only in his patience with those who receive his mercy but his patience with those who don't receive it?

Jonah 4:1-3

"This change of plans greatly upset Jonah, and he became very angry. So he complained to the LORD about it: 'Didn't I say before I left home that you would do this, Lord? That is why I ran away to Tarshish! I knew that you are a merciful and compassionate God, slow to get angry and filled with unfailing love. You are eager to turn back from destroying people. Just kill me now, Lord! I'd rather be dead than alive if what I predicted will not happen.' "

Q: Be honest: Does God's patience for others—those who are bugging you—ever get on your nerves or even make you mad? If so, why do you think that is?

My Reflections

My Reflections

A Fruit of the Spirit

We Want God's Patience, But How Do We Get It?

Note to the Hostess:

At this session, you'll be thinking more about what it means to have a fruit of the Spirit...so what snack could be more appropriate than fruit! Serve a fruit platter with fruits such as grapes, strawberries, pineapple, and bananas. And, if you'd like, serve some lemonade or fruit punch, too. You'll prepare the Experience this week, so read through this section and gather the supplies before your session.

Get It...Got It?...Good.

- ◌ fruit platter and beverage, such as lemonade
- ◌ one healthy plant, and a flower or leaf that is dying

Mingling

Enjoy the snacks the hostess has set out, and talk about what you did during the past week to reflect on and experience God's patience.

Before starting, make sure to pray something like this:

> God, thank you for this session where we can learn about how you can transform us to be more like you. In Jesus' name, amen.

Experience

(Note: The hostess will prepare this experience.) In this session, you'll discuss what it means to remain in Jesus and bear fruit. Find one plant that has firm roots and is growing and flourishing. Then find one flower, branch, or leaf that has been severed from its roots and is dying. (If you have a larger group, gather one healthy and one dying plant per every five women.)

Tell the women that you're going to be discussing how we can bear fruit, like patience, when we remain connected to our root—Jesus. Have each woman feel the leaves of the rooted plant and then the petals or leaves of the disconnected flower or branch. Then answer these questions:

Q: What is the plant that is firmly rooted like?

Q: What is the plant that has no roots like?

Q: How do you think this is like us as we try to produce the "fruit" of patience?

the Word

Read Galatians 5:16-23 and John 15:1-5 together.

Galatians 5:16-23

So I say, let the Holy Spirit guide your lives. Then you won't be doing what your sinful nature craves. The sinful nature wants to do evil, which is just the opposite of what the Spirit wants. And the Spirit gives us desires that are the opposite of what the sinful nature desires. These two forces are constantly fighting each other, so you are not free to carry out your good intentions. But when you are directed by the Spirit, you are not under obligation to the law of Moses.

When you follow the desires of your sinful nature, the results are very clear: sexual immorality, impurity, lustful pleasures, idolatry, sorcery, hostility, quarreling, jealousy, outbursts of anger, selfish ambition, dissension, division, envy, drunkenness, wild parties, and other sins like these. Let me tell you again, as I have before, that anyone living that sort of life will not inherit the Kingdom of God.

But the Holy Spirit produces this kind of fruit in our lives: love, joy, peace, patience, kindness, goodness, faithfulness, gentleness, and self-control. There is no law against these things!

John 15:1-5

I am the true grapevine, and my Father is the gardener. He cuts off every branch of mine that doesn't produce fruit, and he prunes the branches that do bear fruit so they will produce even more. You have already been pruned and purified by the message I have given you. Remain in me, and I will remain in you. For a branch cannot produce fruit if it is severed from the vine, and you cannot be fruitful unless you remain in me.

Yes, I am the vine; you are the branches. Those who remain in me, and I in them, will produce much fruit. For apart from me you can do nothing.

a closer look

Read this box anytime to take a deeper look at the verses for this session.

The Bible gives many examples of what Christ's followers will be like if they remain in him. We read in the Bible that we should be patient and kind, not jealous and selfish, and so we simply try *really* hard to be patient and kind. But most times, trying to be good on our own doesn't work. As Jesus reveals in John 15, we can't bear fruit, the fruit of patience, by ourselves; we'll ultimately fail. But if we remain in him, we will bear much fruit. As Galatians 5 reveals, patience is a fruit of the Spirit—what we naturally produce when we live through the Holy Spirit and not ourselves. Patience isn't something we gain simply through our own effort; it's something we possess when we remain in Jesus and live by the Spirit.

scripture discussion questions

In groups of four or five, discuss these questions:

Q: What does it mean for something to be a fruit of something else?

Q: What do you think it means to let the Holy Spirit guide your life as it says in Galatians 5:16?

Q: Jesus says we can't bear fruit unless we remain in him. What does it mean to remain in him?

Q: What has happened in your life when you have tried to be a patient person without help from Jesus or the Holy Spirit?

Q: In light of these verses, how can we become patient women?

Q: What are practical things you can do to remain in Jesus and to live by the Spirit in order to become more like Jesus—full of patience?

Take Action

Let's not just *talk* about living by the Spirit, *let's do it!* Write below how you're going to remain in Christ and live by the Spirit this week. If you're having a hard time thinking of something, choose one of the ideas below. Next week you'll share with one another how you did.

this week

○ I'm going to remain in Christ this week by:

_____

_____

_____

_____

○ Each time I find myself becoming impatient, I'll pray that God will fill me with his Holy Spirit and give me his love and patience.

○ I'm going to read through all of the verses in the Still Thirsty? section to learn more about becoming patient through Christ.

○ Each morning the first moment I'm awake, I'll ask God to help me live by his Spirit that day—to bear the fruit of patience, kindness, and love.

Prayer

End your time together in prayer to your Father.
Read John 15:5 together:

> Yes, I am the vine; you are the branches. Those who remain in me, and I in them, will produce much fruit. For apart from me you can do nothing.

We can't become patient women by ourselves, but God can transform who we are. Thank God for giving you his Spirit, and pray that he would transform each of you as you live through his Spirit to be more like him.

Girlfriend Time

If you want to spend more time together with your girlfriends, how about having fruit fondue? Use the fruit from your snacks, and dip it in melted chocolate. As you enjoy, discuss together times that you have experienced "fruit" like patience, kindness, joy and peace through living by the Spirit.

Still Thirsty?

If you're still thirsty to know more about remaining in Jesus and living by the Spirit, check out these Scriptures.

Luke 6:43-45

"A good tree can't produce bad fruit, and a bad tree can't produce good fruit. A tree is identified by its fruit. Figs are never gathered from thornbushes, and grapes are not picked from bramble bushes. A good person produces good things from the treasury of a good heart, and an evil person produces evil things from the treasury of an evil heart. What you say flows from what is in your heart."

Q: Based on your reactions to people and circumstances, what flows from your heart?

Romans 8:5-6

"Those who are dominated by the sinful nature think about sinful things, but those who are controlled by the Holy Spirit think about things that please the Spirit. So letting your sinful nature control your mind leads to death. But letting the Spirit control your mind leads to life and peace."

Q: If you have your mind set on what the Spirit desires, how do you think you will react the next time you are in a patience-testing situation? Be specific.

Ephesians 3:16-19

"I pray that from his glorious, unlimited resources he will empower you with inner strength through his Spirit. Then Christ will make his home in your hearts as you trust in him. Your roots will grow down into God's love and keep you strong. And may you have the power to understand, as all God's people should, how wide, how long, how high, and how deep his love is. May you experience the love of Christ, though it is too great to understand fully. Then you will be made complete with all the fullness of life and power that comes from God."

Q: What do you think it means to be complete with all the fullness of life and power that comes from God?

Q: What do you think this verse has to do with patience?

Ephesians 5:18-20

"Don't be drunk with wine, because that will ruin your life. Instead, be filled with the Holy Spirit, singing psalms and hymns and spiritual songs among yourselves, and making music to the Lord in your hearts. And give thanks for everything to God the Father in the name of our Lord Jesus Christ."

Q: If you were filled with the Spirit, how would you speak to others…especially those who try your patience?

My Reflections

My Reflections

Patience in the Small Things

Grocery Stores, Traffic Jams, and Long Lines, Oh My!

Note to the Hostess:

This week you'll be thinking more about patience—in all those little situations that bug you, like traffic jams and long lines. Start with a fun experience and snack that will demonstrate how important patience is, with a fondue snack! Read the Experience section for more details.

Get It...Got It?...Good.

- ○ fondue pot with forks, 1 pot per every 4 to 6 women
- ○ meat fondue (see Experience section for recipe)

> **fondue tip**
>
> You may want to have different women in your group bring the ingredients for the fondue. If so, be sure to ask them ahead of time.

Mingling

As you gather, talk together about your experiences last week living by the Spirit.

Before starting, make sure to pray something like this:

God, thank you for bringing each individual woman here tonight. We pray that you would bless our time together as we learn more about patience.

Experience

(Note: The hostess will prepare this experience.) For your snack this week, enjoy a meat fondue together. Prepare the recipe below before your gathering, and then discuss the questions together while you wait for your meat to cook.

Fondue for Six

½ cup soy sauce

2½ tablespoons Worcestershire sauce

1 clove garlic

2 pounds of beef, cut into 2-inch strips

2 cups vegetable oil

dipping sauces (see below)

Combine the soy sauce, Worcestershire sauce, and garlic in a large plastic bag. Add the meat, and mix. Refrigerate for 4 hours. Before serving, pat the meat dry. Heat the oil in the pot to about 375 degrees. Guests will cook the meat in the hot oil on long-handled fondue forks until desired doneness is reached. Serve with dipping sauces, such as mustard, barbecue sauce, horseradish, curry, soy sauce, and teriyaki. (Search through the stuff crammed in your fridge door!)

Have fresh veggies, such as carrots, snap peas, and broccoli, to cook and dip for your non-meat-eating friends.

Q: Do you enjoy waiting for fondue, or does it kind of bug you? Tell why!

Q: What's the danger of being impatient with our snack?

Q: What's the payoff of being patient? Is this like or unlike patience in real life? How?

the Word

Read Proverbs 19:11, 14:29, and 16:32 together.

Proverbs 19:11

Sensible people control their temper; they earn respect by overlooking wrongs.

Proverbs 14:29

People with understanding control their anger; a hot temper shows great foolishness.

Proverbs 16:32

Better to be patient than powerful; better to have self-control than to conquer a city.

a closer look

Read this box anytime to take a deeper look at the verses for this session.

Proverbs 16 says that it's better to be patient than powerful and better to have self-control than to conquer a city. In ancient cultures, a strong warrior would be considered a powerful person. He was one of the most esteemed, valued, and respected people. Military might and power were of seeming paramount importance for the Israelites who were constantly fighting for their territory. But this ancient proverb turned that value on its head and placed patience as an even higher virtue than might. In fact, the Old Testament repeatedly equates hot-temperedness and impatience with being a fool and patience and temperance with being wise.

scripture discussion questions

In groups of four or five, discuss these questions:

Q: What situations in everyday life make you the most impatient?

Q: How do you react when you're impatient? (Do you sigh, snap at people, bottle it up, yell at the car in front of you?) Be honest!

Q: The verses we read equate impatience with folly. Why do you think it's foolish to be impatient?

Q: Proverbs 19 says sensible people overlook wrongs. What's your opinion of this?

Q: What do you think controlling the temper has to do with patience?

Q: In light of these verses and what you read last week about the fruit of the Spirit, what are some practical steps you can take to become a more patient person?

Take Action

Let's not just *talk* about being patient, *let's do it!* Write below how you're going to practice patience this week. If you're having a hard time thinking of something, choose one of the ideas below. Next week you'll share with one another how you did.

this week

○ I'm going to practice patience this week by:

....

....

....

....

○ I'm going to reflect on how being patient might earn me respect. And I'll let the person behind me go first while I'm reflecting.

○ I will meditate on all the verses in the Still Thirsty? section.

○ I'll pray each day before a situation that usually makes me impatient (like driving to work or to school) for God to give me the wisdom to be patient.

Prayer

End your time together in prayer to your Father.
Read Ephesians 4:1-2 together:

> Therefore I, a prisoner for serving the Lord, beg you to lead a life worthy of your calling, for you have been called by God. Always be humble and gentle. Be patient with each other, making allowance for each other's faults because of your love.

Thank God for his calling on your life, and ask him to help you live a life worthy of that calling. Ask him to help you be patient, humble, and gentle as you follow him.

Girlfriend Time

If you want to spend more time together with your girlfriends, continue your fondue night with a chocolate fondue. As you dip, discuss Ephesians 4:1-2 and how being humble, patient, and kind are part of God's calling for your life.

Still Thirsty?

If you're still thirsty to know more about God's patience, check out these Scriptures.

Ecclesiastes 7:8-9

"Finishing is better than starting. Patience is better than pride. Control your temper, for anger labels you a fool."

Q: How are impatience and pride related?

Proverbs 25:28

"A person without self-control is like a city with broken-down walls."

Q: When you are impatient and lack self-control, how are you like a city with broken-down walls?

Proverbs 21:19

"It's better to live alone in the desert than with a quarrelsome, complaining wife."

Q: When you are ill-tempered and impatient, what are you like to live with? Do you think those who live with you might like a change?

1 Peter 4:7

"The end of the world is coming soon. Therefore, be earnest and disciplined in your prayers."

Q: Can you pray when you're impatient? Why or why not?

Titus 1:7-8

"For an elder must live a blameless life. He must not be arrogant or quick-tempered; he must not be a heavy drinker, violent, or dishonest with money.

"Rather, he must enjoy having guests in his home, and he must love what is good. He must live wisely and be just. He must live a devout and disciplined life."

Q: Why do you think in this passage and in 1 Timothy 3, the requirements of being an elder are not being quick-tempered but being self-controlled and temperate?

Proverbs 17:27-28

"A truly wise person uses few words; a person with understanding is even-tempered. Even fools are thought wise when they keep silent; with their mouths shut, they seem intelligent."

Q: Based on your speech, would others judge you impatient, wise, or foolish?

My Reflections

My Reflections

Love Is Patient

Patience With Those We Love Most

Note to the Hostess:

This week you'll discuss together how we are called to be loving and patient toward one another, acting as one another's servants rather than trying to be first. To be an example of this, serve your guests tonight. Have tea or coffee and different kinds of desserts, such as cookies or pie. As guests enter, ask them to have a seat, and ask them what they'd like. Then serve each of them.

Get It...Got It?...Good.

- coffee or tea
- desserts, such as pie or cookies

Mingling

Enjoy the snacks the hostess has served you, and discuss how you did at practicing patience last week.

Before starting, make sure to pray something like this:

God, thank you for this opportunity to learn more about what your Word has to say about patience. We invite you here tonight and pray that you would guide our time together.

Experience

(Note: The hostess will prepare this experience.) Today you'll talk about being patient with those we love—often the ones we are prone to become the most impatient with. Have each person think of a time or situation in which it is or was difficult for her to remain patient with a loved one. In pairs, talk about the situation, and then answer the questions below as partners. (Make sure your examples are honoring to the people you're talking about and not gossip, though!)

Q: Why is it sometimes hardest to be patient with those we love?

Q: How do you think love and patience relate to each other?

the Word

*Read Matthew 18:21-22, 1 Corinthians 13:4-5,
and Mark 10:42-45 together.*

Matthew 18:21-22

Then Peter came to him and asked, "Lord, how often should I forgive some-one who sins against me? Seven times?" "No, not seven times," Jesus replied, "but seventy times seven!"

1 Corinthians 13:4-5

Love is patient and kind. Love is not jealous or boastful or proud or rude. It does not demand its own way. It is not irritable, and it keeps no record of being wronged.

Mark 10:42-45

So Jesus called them together and said, "You know that the rulers in this world lord it over their people, and officials flaunt their authority over those under them. But among you it will be different. Whoever wants to be a leader among you must be your servant, and whoever wants to be first among you must be the slave of everyone else. For even the Son of Man came not to be served but to serve others and to give his life as a ransom for many."

a closer look

Read this box anytime to take a deeper look at the verses for this session.

Last week we read a number of proverbs that turned ancient values on their heads by saying that, for example, being patient was worth more than being powerful. Jesus also turned the values of his time upside down, saying that those who are the greatest aren't to be served by others but are to be the slaves of others. In a time when important households had servants or slaves, this would have been unthinkable.

When we are impatient, we are thinking of ourselves first, as the most important. But even Jesus himself said he came to be the servant of all. An attitude of patience is, at its core, the attitude of Jesus. As Philippians 2:4-7 says,

"Don't look out only for your own interests, but take an interest in others, too. You must have the same attitude that Christ Jesus had. Though he was God, he did not think of equality with God as something to cling to. Instead, he gave up his divine privileges; he took the humble position of a slave and was born as a human being."

scripture discussion questions

In groups of four or five, discuss these questions:

Q: In Matthew 18, Jesus says that when someone sins against us, we should, just as God is slow to anger, forgive seventy times seven! How many times does it take for a friend or family member to offend you before you run out of patience?

Q: If we truly believe that "love is patient," why is it so easy to lose patience with our loved ones?

Q: Love "keeps no record of being wronged." If you truly forgive the past offenses of your loved ones, how will your patience with them change?

Q: Love doesn't demand its own way. When you're not demanding your own way, how does this affect your patience?

Q: Read the passage from Mark 10 again. If we put ourselves last and become the servant of others, how would that affect our patience?

Q: How do you think we can have the kind of love and patience for others that Jesus had, truly putting others first? Be specific.

Take Action

Let's not just *talk* about being patient with others, *let's do it!* Write below how you're going to be patient with those you love this week. If you're having a hard time thinking of something, choose one of the ideas below. Next week you'll share with one another how you did.

this week

○ I'm going to be patient with my loved ones this week by:

....

....

....

....

○ I will remember how many times Jesus said we are to forgive. And if I'm over that limit, I'll keep going!

○ I'm going to actively put others first by choosing to serve them first before helping myself.

○ I'll meditate on the verses in the Still Thirsty? section and pray for God to fill me with his love.

Prayer

End your time together in prayer to your Father.
Read Colossians 3:12 together:

> Since God chose you to be the holy people he loves, you must clothe yourselves with tenderhearted mercy, kindness, humility, gentleness, and patience.

Thank God that you are his women, holy and dearly loved. Pray that he would help each of you to clothe yourselves with patience and love for those around you.

Girlfriend Time

If you want to spend more time together with your girlfriends, practice putting one another first. Take turns giving each other shoulder or hand rubs. While you take turns, talk about a person in your life who is great at putting others first.

Still Thirsty?

If you're still thirsty to know more about God's patience, check out these Scriptures.

Ephesians 4:1-2

"Therefore I, a prisoner for serving the Lord, beg you to lead a life worthy of your calling, for you have been called by God. Always be humble and gentle. Be patient with each other, making allowance for each other's faults because of your love."

Q: What do you think it means to "make allowances for each other's faults"?

1 Thessalonians 5:14

"Brothers and sisters, we urge you to warn those who are lazy. Encourage those who are timid. Take tender care of those who are weak. Be patient with everyone."

Q: We are to be patient with everyone. Who is the hardest for you to be patient with?

Colossians 3:12

"Since God chose you to be the holy people he loves, you must clothe yourselves with tenderhearted mercy, kindness, humility, gentleness, and patience."

Q: How do you think patience relates to mercy, kindness, humility, and gentleness?

Mark 9:34-35

"But they didn't answer, because they had been arguing about which of them was the greatest. He sat down, called the twelve disciples over to him, and said, 'Whoever wants to be first must take last place and be the servant of everyone else.'"

Q: Often when we're impatient, we have a "me first" attitude. How does an attitude of patience help you to serve others better?

Philippians 2:4-7

"Don't look out only for your own interests, but take an interest in others, too. You must have the same attitude that Christ Jesus had. Though he was God, he did not think of equality with God as something to cling to. Instead, he gave up his divine privileges; he took the humble position of a slave and was born as a human being."

Q: How do you think this verse relates to patience?

My Reflections

Patience in God's Timing

This Isn't What We Had Planned...

Note to the Hostess:

This week we'll discuss the kind of patience we need to have when we have to wait for something we really want to happen—like getting married, finding a job, having a baby, or being healed from an illness. Have some simple snacks for women before your meeting, like hot chocolate and strawberries. Read through the Experience section before your meeting, and gather the supplies you'll need.

Get It...Got It?...Good.

- ○ simple snacks, like hot chocolate and strawberries
- ○ construction paper
- ○ markers

Mingling

Enjoy the snacks the hostess has set out, and discuss how you did last week with being patient with those you love.

Before starting, make sure to pray something like this:

> Dear Lord, we thank you that we know we can put our hope and trust in you, even as we have to wait patiently in this life. Please use your Word to help us understand this better tonight.

Experience

(Note: The hostess will prepare this experience.) Our lives seldom turn out how we plan them. Often God's timing and path for us is very different than what we would have planned ourselves. Each woman should make a parallel-life timeline. Take a piece of construction paper and a marker. Draw one line that represents what *you* had planned—what you were going to do after graduation, when you were going to get a job, and so on. Draw a parallel line that represents what actually happened. Then in small groups or pairs, share your parallel-life timelines.

Q: How do your two lines vary?

Q: Now looking back, are you glad things turned out the way they did or not? Explain.

the Word

Read Ecclesiastes 3:1-8, 11, Lamentations 3:24-26,
and Psalm 27:13-14 together.

Ecclesiastes 3:1-8, 11

For everything there is a season, a time for every activity under heaven. A time to be born and a time to die. A time to plant and a time to harvest. A time to kill and a time to heal. A time to tear down and a time to build up. A time to cry and a time to laugh. A time to grieve and a time to dance. A time to scatter stones and a time to gather stones. A time to embrace and a time to turn away. A time to search and a time to quit searching. A time to keep and a time to throw away. A time to tear and a time to mend. A time to be quiet and a time to speak. A time to love and a time to hate. A time for war and a time for peace.

Yet God has made everything beautiful for its own time. He has planted eternity in the human heart, but even so, people cannot see the whole scope of God's work from beginning to end.

Lamentations 3:24-26

I say to myself, "The Lord is my inheritance; therefore, I will hope in him!" The Lord is good to those who depend on him, to those who search for him. So it is good to wait quietly for salvation from the Lord.

Psalm 27:13-14

Yet I am confident I will see the Lord's goodness while I am here in the land of the living. Wait patiently for the Lord. Be brave and courageous. Yes, wait patiently for the Lord.

a closer look

Read this box anytime to take a deeper look at the verses for this session.

As we see in this week's verses and as most of us can testify from our own lives, often God's timing is not our own. We can't fathom God's plans for us, and it's so hard to wait patiently for them sometimes. David was one man who didn't know what the future held for him—whether or not he was going to be killed by Saul or become king. The Psalms are a record of his cries to God—pleading for help over and over but at the same time stating that his hope and his trust are in God. (See the Still Thirsty? section for a number of these verses.) The psalms help us understand what to do when we have to wait for something and we don't know what will happen: Trust in God, put your hope in him, and wait patiently for him.

scripture discussion questions

In groups of four or five, discuss these questions:

Q: What have you *really* wanted to happen, but you've had to wait for it?

Q: When is it hardest for you to be patient waiting for God's plan for your life?

Q: What does it mean to you that "God has made everything beautiful in its own time"?

Q: What does the passage from Ecclesiastes teach you about waiting?

Q: In Lamentations, it says that God is our inheritance. How does knowing this help you to wait patiently?

Q: Psalm 27:14 says, "Wait patiently for the Lord. Be brave and courageous. Yes, wait patiently for the Lord." How do all the verses you have read about God's timing help you to be strong, take heart, and wait?

Q: What's a practical step you can take to help you wait on God?

Take Action

Let's not just *talk* about waiting on God, *let's do it!* Write below how you're going to wait patiently on God this week. If you're having a hard time thinking of something, choose one of the ideas below. Next week you'll share with one another how you did.

this week

○ I'm going to wait on God this week by:

....

....

....

....

○ Each time I feel frustrated at the circumstances of my life, I'll remember that God is my inheritance and thank him for his plan for my life.

○ I'll review my timeline for my life and the one that reflects God's plan for my life and see how these verses help me understand God better.

○ I will put my requests before God each day and ask him to help me put my hope and trust in him.

Prayer

End your time together in prayer to your Father.
Read Psalm 27:14 together:

> Wait patiently for the Lord. Be brave and courageous. Yes, wait patiently for the Lord.

Thank God that even when we're waiting in a place we don't want to be, we know we can put our hope in him. Ask that he would help each of you to take heart as you wait on him.

Girlfriend Time

If you want to spend more time together with your girlfriends, watch the movie *Sense and Sensibility*. In this movie, Elinor waits for something that she doesn't know will ever happen. Afterward, discuss whether you think you could have her kind of patience.

Still Thirsty?

If you're still thirsty to know more about God's patience, check out these Scriptures:

Micah 7:7

"As for me, I look to the Lord for help. I wait confidently for God to save me, and my God will certainly hear me."

Q: When you're waiting on God, do you believe that he hears you? Why or why not?

Psalm 33:20-22

"We put our hope in the Lord. He is our help and our shield. In him our hearts rejoice, for we trust in his holy name. Let your unfailing love surround us, LORD, for our hope is in you alone."

Q: In what way is the Lord your shield as you wait for him?

Psalm 5:1-3

"O Lord, hear me as I pray; pay attention to my groaning. Listen to my cry for help, my King and my God, for I pray to no one but you. Listen to my voice in the morning, Lord. Each morning I bring my requests to you and wait expectantly."

Q: What is the importance of prayer as we wait on God?

Psalm 37:3-7

"Trust in the Lord and do good. Then you will live safely in the land and prosper. Take delight in the Lord, and he will give you your heart's desires. Commit everything you do to the Lord. Trust him, and he will help you. He will make your innocence radiate like the dawn, and the justice of your cause will shine like the noonday sun. Be still in the presence of the Lord, and wait patiently for him to act."

Q: What do you think it means to "be still" before God? How would you rate yourself on a "be still" meter?

Isaiah 55:8-9

"My thoughts are nothing like your thoughts," says the Lord. "And my ways are far beyond anything you could imagine. For just as the heavens are higher than the earth, so my ways are higher than your ways and my thoughts higher than your thoughts."

Q: How does this verse comfort you as you wait on God?

My Reflections

Patient to the End

Be Patient and Stand Firm

Note to the Hostess:

At your last session together, you're going to reflect on what the Bible has to say about patient perseverance in the faith and in experiencing trials. Read through the Experience section to find out how you'll encourage Christians around the world who are currently persevering through trials. If in accordance with your beliefs, instead of snacks, consider taking part in the Lord's Supper together to remember the inheritance and hope you have in Christ.

Get It...Got It?...Good.

- ◯ stationery and pens for each woman
- ◯ printout of phrases to write to prisoners (see Experience section)
- ◯ a few Bibles so women can do additional reading if they're unfamiliar with some of the people mentioned in this study
- ◯ elements for the Lord's Supper (optional)

Mingling

Discuss with one another how you practiced patience in God's timing last week.

Before starting, make sure to pray something like this:

Dear Lord, we thank you for the inheritance we have in your Son. We pray that you would empower us to patiently endure in our faith in him until the day of his coming.

Experience

(Note: The hostess will prepare this experience.) You and your girlfriends tonight can help encourage Christians enduring persecution around the world. Go to prisoneralert.com to find the names of Christians in other countries who have been imprisoned for their faith. Have stationery and pens available for all the women to write short letters of encouragement to prisoners. The website will give you the addresses you need and instructions on what phrases to write. Before your meeting, print out sheets with phrases the website recommends to write to prisoners. As you open your time, read together Romans 5:3-5:

We can rejoice, too, when we run into problems and trials, for we know that they help us develop endurance. And endurance develops strength of character, and character strengthens our confident hope of salvation. And this hope will not lead to disappointment. For we know how dearly God loves us, because he has given us the Holy Spirit to fill our hearts with his love.

Today you're going to reflect on what the Bible has to say about patient perseverance in the faith. Although many Christians today do not have to face imprisonment or beatings for their faith, many still do. (If you want to re-search more about this, go to persecu-tion.com.) To encourage Christians en-during persecution to persevere, you're going to write letters to them. After you've written the letters, pray together for each of the people you wrote to.

the Word

Read Hebrews 6:10-15 and James 5:7-8 and 10-11 together.

Hebrews 6:10-15

For God is not unjust. He will not forget how hard you have worked for him and how you have shown your love to him by caring for other believers, as you still do. Our great desire is that you will keep on loving others as long as life lasts, in order to make certain that what you hope for will come true. Then you will not become spiritually dull and indifferent. Instead, you will follow the example of those who are going to inherit God's promises because of their faith and endurance.

James 5:7-8, 10-11

Dear brothers and sisters, be patient as you wait for the Lord's return. Consider the farmers who patiently wait for the rains in the fall and in the spring. They eagerly look for the valuable harvest to ripen. You, too, must be patient. Take courage, for the coming of the Lord is near.

For examples of patience in suffering, dear brothers and sisters, look at the prophets who spoke in the name of the Lord. We give great honor to those who endure under suffering. For instance, you know about Job, a man of great endurance. You can see how the Lord was kind to him at the end, for the Lord is full of tenderness and mercy.

a closer look

Read this box anytime to take a deeper look at the verses for this session.

Many times when we hear the word *patience*, the first thing that comes to mind isn't necessarily being patient in persecution and enduring in our faith. Many of us are blessed not to face the kinds of persecution the Early Church did. But a large number of the verses in the New Testament that mention patience don't speak simply about patience with long lines or crying children but patience in trials and persecutions. Out of the 19 verses in the New Testament that speak about our patience (versus God's patience), 11 are specifically about patient endurance in our faith and in trials. (Read through the verses in the Still Thirsty? section to reflect on just a few of these.) New Testament patience is about persevering in our faith and enduring until the Lord's return.

scripture discussion questions

In groups of four or five, discuss these questions:

Q: Discuss how Abraham showed patient endurance while waiting for God's promises. (Need help? Read Genesis 17:1-6 and 21:1-5.)

Q: How do you think you can have the same faith and patience as Abraham, who waited many years before God's promises came true?

Q: Hebrews 6 says, "Our great desire is that you will keep on loving others as long as life lasts, in order to make certain that what you hope for will come true." What do you think this verse means for your own life?

Q: Have someone in your group explain how Job patiently endured through trials. (Need help? Read Job 1:13-19, 2:7-10, and 13:15.)

Q: Do you think you could have had as much perseverance as Job, still praising God though he experienced so many awful trials?

Q: After telling about Job's patient endurance, James 5 points out that the Lord is full of tenderness and mercy. How does knowing this help you persevere and endure in trials?

Q: As a follower of Christ, in what areas in your own life do you think you need to have patient endurance as you wait for the coming of the Lord?

Q: James 5 says, "You, too, must be patient. Take courage, for the coming of the Lord is near." What practical step can you take to stand firm in patience and faith until the day of the Lord's coming?

Take Action

Let's not just *talk* about patiently enduring until Christ's return, *let's do it!* Write below how you're going to patiently endure this week. If you're having a hard time thinking of something, choose one of the ideas below.

| this week |

○ I'm going to patiently endure in faith this week by:

....

....

....

○ I will read through the book of Hebrews and reflect on the faith of other heroes of the faith who have patiently persevered.

○ I'm going to spend time praying for those around the world who are persevering through persecution and hardship. (Check out these two websites: persecution.com and win1040.com.)

○ I will read Colossians 1:10-12 each morning to remind myself of why I am patiently enduring in my faith.

○ I'll reflect on the verses in the Still Thirsty? section to learn more about patient endurance.

Prayer

End your time together in prayer to your Father.
Read Colossians 1:10-12 together:

> Then the way you live will always honor and please the Lord, and your lives will produce every kind of good fruit. All the while, you will grow as you learn to know God better and better.
>
> We also pray that you will be strengthened with all his glorious power so you will have all the endurance and patience you need. May you be filled with joy, always thanking the Father. He has enabled you to share in the inheritance that belongs to his people, who live in the light.

God's Word asks us to patiently endure, as we thank him for our inheritance in him. Thank God for the incredible inheritance you have in Christ, and pray that he would empower you to patiently endure in faith until Christ's return.

Girlfriend Time

If you want to spend more time together with your girlfriends, spend time talking about what God has revealed to you over the past several weeks. Have each friend share the biggest thing she learned or wants to apply from your time studying patience together.

simply relevant | SAVOR THE MOMENTS

Still Thirsty?

If you're still thirsty to know more about God's patience, check out these Scriptures.

Romans 8:22-25

"For we know that all creation has been groaning as in the pains of childbirth right up to the present time. And we believers also groan, even though we have the Holy Spirit within us as a foretaste of future glory, for we long for our bodies to be released from sin and suffering. We, too, wait with eager hope for the day when God will give us our full rights as his adopted children, including the new bodies he has promised us. We were given this hope when we were saved. (If we already have something, we don't need to hope for it. But if we look forward to something we don't yet have, we must wait patiently and confidently.)"

Q: How does your hope in Christ's salvation make you more patient?

James 1:2-4

"Dear brothers and sisters, when troubles come your way, consider it an opportunity for great joy. For you know that when your faith is tested, your endurance has a chance to grow. So let it grow, for when your endurance is fully developed, you will be perfect and complete, needing nothing."

Q: How can you put this verse into practice—to consider it an opportunity for great joy when troubles come your way? Think of a few really specific things you can do.

1 Thessalonians 1:3

"As we pray to our God and Father about you, we think of your faithful work, your loving deeds, and the enduring hope you have because of our Lord Jesus Christ."

Q: What inspires you to have enduring hope?

2 Corinthians 1:3-6

"All praise to God, the Father of our Lord Jesus Christ. God is our merciful Father and the source of all comfort. He comforts us in all our troubles so that we can comfort others. When they are troubled, we will be able to give them the same comfort God has given us. For the more we suffer for Christ, the more God will shower us with his comfort through Christ. Even when we are weighed down with troubles, it is for your comfort and salvation! For when we ourselves are comforted, we will certainly comfort you. Then you can patiently endure the same things we suffer."

Q: Think on a time when you suffered and later realized that time had produced in you patient endurance? How do you feel about that time, looking back on it now?

Hebrews 10:36-37

"Patient endurance is what you need now, so that you will continue to do God's will. Then you will receive all that he has promised. 'For in just a little while, the Coming One will come and not delay.' "

Q: Is there an area in your life in which you're struggling to do God's will? Which verses that we've studied can help you in this area?

James 1:12

"God blesses those who patiently endure testing and temptation. Afterward they will receive the crown of life that God has promised to those who love him."

Q: Is there a trial in your life you need to patiently endure? Who can you talk to and pray with through this time?

My Reflections

My Reflections